Cruise through French vocab with CGP!

If you're aiming for a *bon voyage* through GCSE French,
this nifty CGP Vocab Book is just the ticket.

It covers all the key words you'll need for every topic, with handy
tick boxes to help you keep track of which ones you've learned.

It may be small, but it's perfect for making sure your
GCSE French journey doesn't end in Rouen...

CGP — still the best! ☺

Our sole aim here at CGP is to produce the highest quality books —
carefully written, immaculately presented and dangerously close to being funny.

Then we work our socks off to get them out to you
— at the cheapest possible prices.

Contents

Section 1 — General

Section 2 — Identity & Culture

Contents

Published by CGP

Editors:
Rose Jones
Louise McEvoy
Hannah Roscoe
Matt Topping

With thanks to Claire Boulter and Cathy Lear for the proofreading.
With thanks to Jan Greenway for the copyright research.

ISBN: 978 1 78294 861 2

Printed by Elanders Ltd, Newcastle upon Tyne.

Clipart from Corel®

Colours

blanc	*white*	noir	*black*
bleu	*blue*	noisette	*hazel*
blond	*blond*	pourpre	*purple*
brun	*brown*	rose	*pink*
clair	*light*	rouge	*red*
foncé	*dark*	roux	*red (hair)*
gris	*grey*	vert	*green*
jaune	*yellow*	violet	*purple*
marron	*chestnut, brown*		

Higher only:

vif	*bright*

Common and Useful Words

à l'extérieur	*outside*	complètement	*completely*
à moi	*my, mine*	compter	*to count*
autre	*other*	continuer	*to continue*
ça	*that*	d'ailleurs	*besides*
Also cela		de la part de	*on behalf of*
celui-ci	*this one*	doucement	*softly, quietly,*
celui-là	*that one*		*slowly*
chacun	*each (one)*	s'échapper	*to escape*
changer	*to change*	l'entrée libre *(f)*	*free entry*
chaque	*each*	fermer	*to close*
la chose	*thing*	informer	*to inform*
Also le truc		la manière	*manner, way*
complet	*full (no more room)*	le mot	*word*

noter	*to note*	rendre	*to give back, to make (+ adjective)*
occupé	*occupied*		
ouvert	*open*	se rendre compte	*to realise*
ouvrir	*to open*	signifier	*to mean*
par hasard	*by chance*	surtout	*especially, above all*
particulier	*particular, individual*		
		tenir	*to hold*
quelque chose	*something*	très	*very*
quelqu'un	*someone*		

Higher only:

les connaissances *(f)* knowledge

Comparing Things

beaucoup	*a lot*	mauvais	*bad*
bien	*well*	même	*same*
bon	*good*	moins	*less*
le moins	*the least*	moins que	*less than*
le plus	*the most*	plus	*more*
mal	*badly*	plus que	*more than*

Higher only:

autant	*as much*	le plus mal	*the worst (adverb)*
le meilleur	*the best (adjective)*	meilleur	*better (adjective)*
le mieux	*the best (adverb)*	mieux	*better (adverb)*
le pire	*the worst (adjective)*	pire	*worse (adjective)*
		plus mal	*worse (adverb)*

Conjunctions

à cause de	*because of*	évidemment	*evidently, obviously*
à part	*apart (from)*		
afin que	*so that*	mais	*but*
ainsi	*thus, in this way*	même si	*even if*
alors	*then, so*	ou	*or*
au moins	*at least*	par contre	*on the other hand*
aussi	*also*		
car	*because, as*	par exemple	*for example*
cependant	*however*	parce que	*because*
c'est-à-dire	*that's to say*	pendant que	*while*
comme	*as, like*	pourtant	*however*
de l'autre côté	*on the other hand*	puis	*then*
		puisque	*since*
donc	*so, therefore*	sans doute	*without doubt*
d'un côté	*on the one hand*	sauf	*except*
ensuite	*then*	si	*if*
et	*and*	y compris	*including*

Higher only:

dès que	*as soon as*

4

Days, Months and Seasons

lundi	Monday	juin	June
mardi	Tuesday	juillet	July
mercredi	Wednesday	août	August
jeudi	Thursday	septembre	September
vendredi	Friday	octobre	October
samedi	Saturday	novembre	November
dimanche	Sunday	décembre	December
janvier	January	le printemps	spring
février	February	l'été *(m)*	summer
mars	March	l'automne *(m)*	autumn
avril	April	l'hiver *(m)*	winter
mai	May		

Greetings and Exclamations

à bientôt	*see you soon*	bon anniversaire!	*happy birthday!*
à demain	*see you tomorrow*	bon appétit!	*enjoy your meal!*
		bon courage!	*good luck!*
à plus tard	*see you later*	*Also* bonne chance!	
Also à tout à l'heure		bon séjour!	*enjoy your stay!*
allô!	*hello! (on phone)*	bon voyage!	*enjoy your trip!*
amitiés	*best wishes, yours*	bonjour	*hello, good day*
attention!	*look out!*	Bonne année!	*Happy New Year!*
au revoir	*goodbye*	bonne chance!	*good luck!*
au secours!	*help!*	bonne idée!	*good idea!*
bien sûr	*of course*	bonne journée	*have a good day*
bienvenue!	*welcome!*	bonne nuit	*good night*

bonne soirée	have a good evening	Mesdames	ladies
bonnes vacances!	have a good holiday!	Messieurs	gentlemen
		non	no
bonsoir	good evening	oui	yes
bravo!	well done!	pardon	sorry, pardon
ça va	I'm fine	quel dommage!	what a shame!
comme ci comme ça	so-so	salut!	hi!
d'accord	okay	santé!	cheers!
de rien	you're welcome, it's nothing	si!	yes! (after negative)
désolé	sorry	s'il te plaît	please (informal)
excusez-moi	I'm sorry, excuse me	s'il vous plaît	please (formal)
		tant mieux!	all the better!
félicitations!	congratulations!	tant pis!	too bad! never mind!
je t'en prie Also je vous en prie	it's a pleasure	voici	here you are
joyeux Noël	Merry Christmas	voilà	there you are
meilleurs voeux	best wishes	zut!	damn!
merci	thank you		

Higher only:

se serrer la main	to shake hands

Materials

l'argent *(m)*	*silver*	le métal	*metal*
le béton	*concrete*	l'or *(m)*	*gold*
le bois	*wood*	le papier	*paper*
le carton	*cardboard*	la pierre	*stone*
le coton	*cotton*	le plastique	*plastic*
le cuir	*leather*	le plomb	*lead*
le fer	*iron*	la soie	*silk*
la laine	*wool*	le verre	*glass*

Negatives

moi non plus	*me neither*	ne…que	*only*
ne…jamais	*never*	ne…rien	*nothing*
ne…personne	*no-one, nobody*	ni…ni	*neither…nor*
ne…plus	*no longer*	pas encore	*not yet*
ne…pas	*not*	pas grand-chose	*not much*

Numbers

un	one	le mille	thousand
deux	two	le million	million
trois	three	premier	first
quatre	four	deuxième	second
cinq	five	troisième	third
six	six	quatrième	fourth
sept	seven	cinquième	fifth
huit	eight	sixième	sixth
neuf	nine	septième	seventh
dix	ten	huitième	eighth
onze	eleven	neuvième	ninth
douze	twelve	dixième	tenth
treize	thirteen	la centaine	about a hundred
quatorze	fourteen	le chiffre	number (graphical figure)
quinze	fifteen		
seize	sixteen	la dizaine	about ten
dix-sept	seventeen	la douzaine	dozen
dix-huit	eighteen	le nombre	number (amount)
dix-neuf	nineteen	nombre de	several, a good number of
vingt	twenty		
trente	thirty	nombreux	numerous
quarante	forty	le numéro	number (e.g. phone number)
cinquante	fifty		
soixante	sixty	pas mal de	quite a few
soixante-dix	seventy	plusieurs	several
quatre-vingts	eighty	tous les deux	both
quatre-vingt-dix	ninety	tout	all
cent	hundred	la vingtaine	about twenty

Higher only:

ajouter	to add

8

à mon avis	in my opinion	désagréable	unpleasant
absolument	absolutely	désirer	to want, to desire
affreux	awful	détester	to hate
agréable	nice	la différence	difference
aimer	to like, to love	différent	different
amusant	fun, amusing	difficile	difficult
avec plaisir	with pleasure	dire	to say
avoir de la chance	to be lucky	d'une grande valeur	valuable
bien entendu	of course, as a matter of course	efficace	effective, efficient
ça dépend	it depends	embêtant	annoying, frustrating
ça me fait rire	that makes me laugh	en avoir marre	to have had enough
ça me plaît	I like that	en général	in general
ça m'énerve	it gets on my nerves	enchanté	delighted (to meet you)
ça m'est égal	I don't mind	ennuyeux	boring
ça ne fait rien	it doesn't matter	Also barbant	
ça ne me dit rien	I don't fancy that, I don't want to	épouvantable	dreadful, appalling
ça suffit	that's enough	espérer	to hope
casse-pieds	annoying, a pain in the neck	étonné	surprised, astonished
ce n'est pas la peine	it's not worth it	excellent	excellent
certain	certain, sure	extraordinaire	extraordinary
cher	dear, expensive	facile	easy
chouette	great	faible	weak
comme ci comme ça	so-so	fanatique de	fanatical about
compliqué	complicated	fantastique	fantastic
content	pleased	formidable	great, marvellous
croire	to believe, to think	franchement	honestly
		généralement	generally

génial	*brilliant*	personnellement	*personally*
grave	*serious*	pessimiste	*pessimistic*
habile	*clever, skilful*	peut-être	*perhaps*
heureusement	*fortunately*	plutôt	*rather*
idéal	*ideal*	populaire	*popular*
incroyable	*unbelievable*	positif	*positive*
inquiet	*worried*	pratique	*practical*
intéressant	*interesting*	préféré	*favourite*
s'intéresser à	*to be interested in*	Also favori	
		préférer	*to prefer*
inutile	*useless*	promettre	*to promise*
j'en ai assez	*I've had enough*	regretter	*to regret, to be sorry*
Also j'en ai marre			
joyeux	*merry, joyous*	ridicule	*ridiculous*
magnifique	*magnificent*	satisfait	*satisfied*
malheureusement	*unfortunately*	sembler	*to seem*
marrant	*funny*	sensass	*sensational*
merveilleux	*amazing, marvellous*	simple	*simple*
		stupide	*stupid*
mignon	*cute, sweet*	super	*great*
moche	*ugly, ghastly*	superbe	*superb*
moderne	*modern*	supporter	*to bear, to cope with*
nouveau	*new*		
nul	*no good*	surpris	*surprised*
optimiste	*optimistic*	trouver	*to find*
passionnant	*exciting*	utile	*useful*
la peine	*grief, trouble, effort*	volontiers	*with pleasure*
		vouloir	*to want*
penser	*to think*	vraiment	*really*

Higher only:

l'avis *(m)*	*opinion*	la perte de temps	*waste of time*
être d'accord	*to agree*		

Section 1 — General

Parts of the Body

la bouche	*mouth*	la main	*hand*
le bras	*arm*	le nez	*nose*
le cerveau	*brain*	l'ongle *(f)*	*nail*
les cheveux *(m)*	*hair*	l'oreille *(f)*	*ear*
le coeur	*heart*	l'os *(m)*	*bone*
le corps	*body*	la peau	*skin*
le cou	*neck*	le pied	*foot*
la dent	*tooth*	le sang	*blood*
le doigt	*finger*	la tête	*head*
le dos	*back*	le ventre	*tummy*
l'estomac *(m)*	*stomach*	le visage	*face*
la jambe	*leg*	*Also* la figure	
les lèvres *(f)*	*lips*	la voix	*voice*

Higher only:

le coude	*elbow*	l'oeil *(m)*	*eye*
l'épaule *(f)*	*shoulder*	l'orteil *(m)*	*toe*
le genou	*knee*	*Also* le doigt de pied	
la gorge	*throat*	le poumon	*lung*

Prepositions

à	*at, to*	derrière	*behind*
à côté de	*next to*	devant	*in front (of)*
à partir de	*from (a date or time)*	en	*in, by*
		en dehors de	*outside*
à travers	*across*	en face de	*opposite*
au bord de	*alongside*	entre	*between*
au bout de	*at the end of*	loin de	*far from*
au fond de	*at the bottom of*	malgré	*despite, in spite of*
au lieu de	*instead of*		
au milieu de	*in the middle of*	parmi	*among*
au premier plan	*in the foreground*	pour	*for, in order to*
au-dessous de	*underneath*	près de	*near (to)*
au-dessus de	*above*	sans	*without*
autour de	*around*	selon	*according to*
avec	*with*	*Also* d'après	
contre	*against*	sous	*under*
dans	*in(side)*	sur	*on*
de	*of, from*	vers	*towards, approximately*
depuis	*since*		

12

Questions

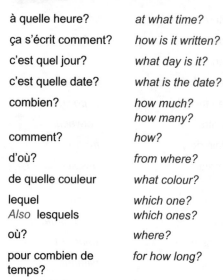

à quelle heure?	*at what time?*	qu'est-ce que?	*what?*
ça s'écrit comment?	*how is it written?*	qu'est-ce que c'est?	*what is it?*
c'est quel jour?	*what day is it?*	qu'est-ce que cela veut dire?	*what does that mean?*
c'est quelle date?	*what is the date?*		
combien?	*how much?* *how many?*	qu'est-ce qui?	*what?*
		quand?	*when?*
comment?	*how?*	que?	*what?*
d'où?	*from where?*	que veut dire...?	*what does... mean?*
de quelle couleur	*what colour?*		
lequel *Also* lesquels	*which one?* *which ones?*	quel?	*what? which?*
		quelle heure est-il?	*what time is it?*
où?	*where?*	qui?	*who?*
pour combien de temps?	*for how long?*	quoi?	*what?*
pourquoi?	*why?*		

Right and Wrong

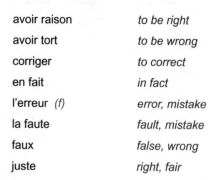

avoir raison	*to be right*	nécessaire	*necessary*
avoir tort	*to be wrong*	obligatoire	*obligatory*
corriger	*to correct*	parfait	*perfect*
en fait	*in fact*	sûr	*sure*
l'erreur *(f)*	*error, mistake*	se tromper	*to be wrong, to make a mistake*
la faute	*fault, mistake*		
faux	*false, wrong*	vrai	*true*
juste	*right, fair*		

Shapes, Weights and Measures

assez	*enough, quite*	le litre	*litre*
bas	*low*	mesurer	*to measure*
beaucoup de	*much, many, a lot of*	le mètre	*metre*
		mince	*thin*
la boîte	*tin, box, can*	la moitié	*half*
la bouteille	*bottle*	le morceau	*piece*
carré	*square*	moyen	*average, middle, medium*
le centilitre	*centilitre*		
le centimètre	*centimetre*	le paquet	*packet*
le cercle	*circle*	peser	*to weigh*
court	*short*	petit	*small, short*
la douzaine	*dozen*	peu	*little*
dur	*hard*	plein	*full*
encore	*more*	la pointure	*shoe size*
étroit	*narrow*	le pot	*jar*
la forme	*shape*	quelques	*some*
le gramme	*gram*	rond	*round*
haut	*high*	suffisamment	*enough, sufficiently*
le hauteur	*height*		
le kilo	*kilo, kilogram*	la taille	*size*
le kilomètre	*kilometre*	le tiers	*third (fraction)*
large	*wide*	la tranche	*slice*
léger	*light*	trop	*too*

Higher only:

à peine	*hardly*	lourd	*heavy*

Time Expressions

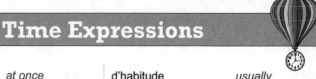

à la fois	*at once*
à l'avenir	*in the future*
à l'heure	*on time*
à temps partiel	*part time*
actuel	*present, current*
actuellement	*at the present time, currently*
l'an *(m)* Also l'année *(f)*	*year*
après	*after*
après-demain	*the day after tomorrow*
l'après-midi *(m)*	*afternoon*
au début	*at the start*
aujourd'hui	*today*
auparavant	*beforehand*
autrefois	*formerly*
avant	*before*
avant-hier	*the day before yesterday*
bientôt	*soon*
d'abord	*first of all*
la date	*date*
de bonne heure	*on time, early*
de nouveau	*again, once more*
de temps en temps	*from time to time*
le début	*start, beginning*
déjà	*already*
demain	*tomorrow*
demi	*half*
dernier	*last*
deux fois	*twice*

d'habitude	*usually*
durer	*to last*
en attendant	*in the meantime*
en avance	*in advance*
en ce moment	*at the moment*
en même temps	*at the same time*
en retard	*late (for something)*
en train de	*in the process of*
encore une fois	*once again*
enfin	*finally, at last*
environ	*about*
être en train de	*to be in the process of*
être sur le point de	*to be about to*
la fin	*end*
finalement	*finally*
la fois	*time (occurrence)*
hebdomadaire	*weekly*
l'heure *(f)*	*hour, time*
hier	*yesterday*
il y a	*ago*
l'instant *(m)*	*moment, instant*
le jour Also la journée	*day*
jusqu'à	*until*
le lendemain	*the next day*
longtemps	*(for) a long time*
maintenant	*now*
le matin	*morning*
la matinée	*morning*
mensuel	*monthly*

midi	*noon, lunchtime*	la saison	*season*
minuit	*midnight*	la seconde	*second*
la minute	*minute*	la semaine	*week*
le mois	*month*	seulement	*only*
normalement	*normally*	le siècle	*century*
la nuit	*night*	le soir	*evening*
passé	*last, just gone*	*Also* la soirée	
le passé	*past*	soudain	*sudden(ly)*
pendant	*during*	souvent	*often*
plus tard	*later*	suivant	*following*
pour l'instant	*for the moment*	sur le point de	*on the point of*
presque	*almost*	tard	*late*
prochain	*next*	tôt	*early*
le quart	*quarter*	toujours	*always, still*
quelquefois	*sometimes*	tous les jours	*every day*
Also parfois		tout à coup	*all of a sudden,*
la quinzaine	*fortnight*	*Also* tout d'un coup	*suddenly*
Also les quinze jours *(m)*		tout de suite	*straight away*
		une fois	*once*
rarement	*rarely*	la veille	*day before, eve*
récemment	*recently*	vite	*quickly*
récent	*recent*	le week-end	*weekend*
le retard	*delay*		

Higher only:

instantané	*instantaneous*	venir de	*to have just*

Abbreviations

la BD (bande-dessinée)	comic book
le CDI (centre de documentation et d'information)	school library
le CES (collège d'enseignement secondaire)	secondary school
les DOM *(m)* (départements d'outre-mer)	French departments overseas
l'EMT *(f)* (éducation manuelle et technique)	D&T, CDT
l'EPS *(f)* (éducation physique et sportive)	PE
l'HLM *(f)* (habitation à loyer modéré)	council flat, council house
la MJC (maison des jeunes et de la culture)	youth club and arts centre
P et T	post office and tele-communications service

le RER (réseau express régional)	commuter train service
la RN (route nationale)	main road
le SAMU (service d'aide médicale d'urgence)	ambulance service
le SDF (sans domicile fixe)	homeless person
la SNCF (société nationale des chemins de fer français)	French national railway company
SVP (s'il vous plaît)	please
le TGV (train à grande vitesse)	high speed train
la TVA (taxe sur valeur ajoutée)	VAT
l'UE *(f)* (Union Européenne)	EU
le VTT (vélo tout terrain)	mountain bike, mountain biking

Animals

l'animal *(m)*	animal	la mouche	fly
l'animal domestique *(m)*	pet	le mouton	sheep
le chat	cat	l'oiseau *(m)*	bird
le cheval	horse	le poisson rouge	goldfish
le chien	dog	le poisson tropical	tropical fish
le cochon	pig	le serpent	snake
le cochon d'Inde	guinea pig	la souris	mouse
le hamster	hamster	la tortue	tortoise
le lapin	rabbit	la vache	cow

Clothes

à la mode	fashionable	la chaussette	sock
à pois	spotty	la chaussure	shoe
l'anneau *(m)*	ring	la chemise	shirt
Also la bague		la chemise de nuit	nightie
les bijoux *(m)*	jewellery	le collant	tights
le blouson	jacket (casual)	le collier	necklace
la botte	boot	le complet	three-piece suit
les boucles d'oreille *(f)*	earrings	la couleur	colour
le bracelet	bracelet	la cravate	tie
le caleçon	boxers	la culotte	knickers
la casquette	cap	démodé	old-fashioned
la ceinture	belt	de taille moyenne	medium
le chapeau	hat	l'écharpe *(f)*	scarf

18

enlever *Also* ôter	*to take off,* *to remove*	le piercing à l'oreille	*ear piercing*
les fringues *(f)*	*clothes*	la poche	*pocket*
le gant	*glove*	le polo	*polo shirt*
le gilet	*cardigan*	le pull	*sweater, jumper*
il te va bien	*it suits you*	le pyjama	*pyjamas*
l'imper(méable) *(m)*	*waterproof*	rayé	*stripy*
le jean	*jeans*	rétro	*retro*
la jupe	*skirt*	la robe	*dress*
le lin	*linen*	le rouge à lèvres	*lipstick*
les lunettes de soleil *(f)*	*sunglasses*	le sac	*bag*
le maillot de bain	*swimsuit, trunks*	le sac à main	*handbag*
le maillot de sport	*sports shirt*	le short	*shorts*
le manteau	*coat*	le slip	*underpants*
le maquillage	*make-up*	le soutien-gorge	*bra*
la mode	*fashion*	le style	*style*
la montre	*watch*	le survêtement	*tracksuit*
le mouchoir	*tissue,* *handkerchief*	la tenue de sport	*sports kit*
la paire	*pair*	le tricot	*jumper*
le pantalon	*trousers*	le t-shirt	*T-shirt*
le parapluie	*umbrella*	la veste	*jacket*
		les vêtements *(m)*	*clothes*
		vêtu de	*dressed in*

Higher only:

le casque	*helmet*	se faire couper les cheveux	*to have your hair* *cut*
le chapeau de paille	*straw hat*	le foulard	*scarf*
le chemisier	*blouse*	le képi	*military cap*
le costume	*suit*	se maquiller	*to put on* *make-up*
la couture	*sewing, tailoring*		
emprunter	*to borrow*	les pantoufles *(f)*	*slippers*
se faire coiffer	*to have your hair* *done*	le pull à capuche	*hoody,* *hooded top*

la robe de chambre	*dressing gown*	le trou	*hole*
serré	*tight*	le velours	*velvet*
teint	*dyed*		

Daily Routine

apporter	*to bring*	habituel	*usual*
la brosse à dents	*toothbrush*	laver	*to wash*
se brosser les dents	*to brush your teeth*	se laver	*to have a wash*
commencer	*to begin*	se lever	*to get up, to stand up*
se coucher	*to go to bed*	organiser	*to organise*
le dentifrice	*toothpaste*	se raser	*to shave*
se déshabiller	*to get undressed, to undress*	le réveil	*alarm clock*
		se réveiller	*to wake up*
dormir	*to sleep*	le sèche-cheveux	*hair dryer*
se doucher	*to have a shower*	la serviette	*towel*
faire la cuisine	*to do the cooking*	la vie	*life*
finir	*to finish, to end*		
s'habiller	*to get dressed*		

Higher only:

avoir sommeil	*to be sleepy*	quotidien	*daily*
faire la grasse matinée	*to have a lie in*		

Describing People

avoir	to have	laid	ugly
la barbe	beard	long	long
barbu	bearded	les lunettes (f)	glasses
beau	beautiful	maigre	thin
bouclé	wavy, curly	le mec	guy
la célébrité	celebrity	mi-long	medium length
Also la star		la moustache	moustache
châtain	brown (hair)	musulman	Muslim
chauve	bald	normal	normal
chrétien	Christian	pareil	the same
de bonne humeur	in a good mood	se plaindre	to complain
de mauvaise humeur	in a bad mood	plus âgé	older
décrire	to describe	le poids	weight
en bonne forme	fit	raide	straight (hair)
enceinte	pregnant	reconnu	well-known
être	to be	la religion	religion
le fils unique	only child	sensationnel	sensational
Also la fille unique		Also sensass	
frisé	frizzy, curly	le sens de l'humour	sense of humour
grand	tall	la sorte	type
gros	fat	sourd	deaf
l'humeur (f)	mood	le tatouage	tattoo
joli	pretty	triste	sad
juif	Jewish	les yeux (m)	eyes

Higher only:

élégant	elegant	la foi	faith
l'esprit (m)	wit, intelligence	le genre	type
étonnant	surprising	habillé	dressed
étrange	strange	maladroit	clumsy

se mettre en colère	*to get angry*	retraité	*retired*
le modèle	*role model*	le sexe	*gender*
ondulé	*wavy*	similaire	*similar*
ressembler à	*to look like, to resemble*		

Eating Out

à la carte	*from the menu, à la carte*	le goût	*taste*
		grillé	*grilled*
l'addition *(f)*	*bill*	le hors-d'oeuvre	*starter*
l'alcool *(m)*	*alcohol*	le menu à prix fixe	*fixed price menu*
l'assiette *(f)*	*plate*	le parfum	*flavour*
l'auberge *(f)*	*inn*	partager	*to share*
la bière	*beer*	payer	*to pay*
la boisson	*drink*	la petite cuillère	*teaspoon*
la carte	*menu*	la pizzeria	*pizzeria*
le casse-croûte	*snack*	le plat	*dish*
commander	*to order*	le plat du jour	*dish of the day*
compris	*included*	le plat principal	*main course*
la côtelette	*chop*	le poivre	*pepper*
le couteau	*knife*	le pourboire	*tip*
les couverts *(m)*	*cutlery*	le repas	*meal*
la cuillère Also la cuiller	*spoon*	le restaurant	*restaurant*
		le salon de thé	*tea room*
cuit	*cooked*	le sel	*salt*
le dessert	*dessert*	le self-service	*self-service*
l'entrecôte *(f)*	*steak*	service compris	*service included*
la fourchette	*fork*	service non compris	*service not included*
le glacier	*ice cream parlour*		

servir	*to serve*	le verre	*glass*
la spécialité	*speciality*	le vin	*wine*
le supplément	*supplement*		

Higher only:

à point	*medium (meat)*	épais	*thick*
l'apéritif *(m)*	*aperitif, drink before a meal*	l'huître *(f)*	*oyster*
appétissant	*appetising*	piquant *Also* épicé	*hot, spicy*
bien cuit	*well done (meat)*	le plateau	*tray*
la brasserie	*bar-restaurant*	saignant	*rare (meat)*

Family

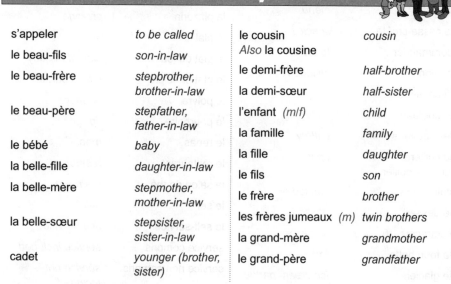

s'appeler	*to be called*	le cousin *Also* la cousine	*cousin*
le beau-fils	*son-in-law*	le demi-frère	*half-brother*
le beau-frère	*stepbrother, brother-in-law*	la demi-sœur	*half-sister*
le beau-père	*stepfather, father-in-law*	l'enfant *(m/f)*	*child*
le bébé	*baby*	la famille	*family*
la belle-fille	*daughter-in-law*	la fille	*daughter*
la belle-mère	*stepmother, mother-in-law*	le fils	*son*
la belle-sœur	*stepsister, sister-in-law*	le frère	*brother*
cadet	*younger (brother, sister)*	les frères jumeaux *(m)*	*twin brothers*
		la grand-mère	*grandmother*
		le grand-père	*grandfather*

les grands-parents *(m)*	*grandparents*	le papa	*dad*
le jumeau	*twin (male)*	le papy	*granddad*
la jumelle	*twin (female)*	*Also* le pépé	
la maman	*mum*	les parents *(m)*	*parents*
la mamie	*grandma*	le père	*father*
Also la mémé		le petit-enfant	*grandchild*
marié	*married*	le petit-fils	*grandson*
se marier	*to get married*	la petite-fille	*granddaughter*
le membre de la famille	*family member*	la responsabilité	*responsibility*
la mère	*mother*	la sœur	*sister*
né le...	*born on the*	les sœurs jumelles *(f)*	*twin sisters*
le neveu	*nephew*	se souvenir de	*to remember*
la nièce	*niece*	la tante	*aunt*
l'oncle *(m)*	*uncle*	unique	*only (child)*
		le voisin	*neighbour*

Higher only:

adopté	*adopted*	la mère célibataire	*single mother*
le baptême	*christening*	le parent	*relation*
le fiancé	*fiancé(e)*	le père célibataire	*single father*
Also la fiancée		surveiller	*to watch, to keep an eye on*
gâter	*to spoil (a child)*		
		les vrais jumeaux *(m)*	*identical twins*

Fruit and Veg

l'abricot *(m)*	*apricot*	le melon	*melon*
l'ananas *(m)*	*pineapple*	l'oignon *(m)*	*onion*
la banane	*banana*	l'orange *(f)*	*orange*
la carotte	*carrot*	le pamplemousse	*grapefruit*
la cerise	*cherry*	la pêche	*peach*
le champignon	*mushroom*	les petits-pois *(m)*	*peas*
le chou	*cabbage*	la poire	*pear*
le chou de Bruxelles	*Brussels sprout*	le poivron	*pepper*
le chou-fleur	*cauliflower*	la pomme	*apple*
le citron	*lemon*	la pomme de terre	*potato*
les crudités *(f)*	*raw vegetables*	pourri	*rotten*
la fraise	*strawberry*	la prune	*plum*
la framboise	*raspberry*	le radis	*radish*
le fruit	*fruit*	le raisin	*grape*
le haricot	*bean*	la salade	*lettuce, salad*
le haricot vert	*green bean*	la tomate	*tomato*
le légume	*vegetable*		

Higher only:

l'ail *(m)*	*garlic*	la laitue	*lettuce*
l'artichaut *(m)*	*artichoke*	mûr	*ripe*
le concombre	*cucumber*	le poireau	*leek*
les épinards	*spinach*		

Going Out

à l'appareil	on the line, speaking	immédiatement	immediately
appeler	to call	l'invitation (f)	invitation
arriver	to arrive	inviter	to invite
le bar	bar	raconter	to tell
la boîte de nuit	nightclub	remettre	to put back, to postpone
le coup de téléphone	telephone call	rencontrer	to meet
se dépêcher	to hurry	rendre visite à	to visit (a person)
la discothèque	disco	sonner	to ring
entendre	to hear	téléphoner	to phone
le faux numéro	wrong number		

Higher only:

annuler	to cancel	l'événement (m)	event
le bip sonore	tone	le feu d'artifice	fireworks
le combiné	receiver	l'indicatif (m)	area code
composer le numéro	to dial the number	la messagerie vocale	voice mail

Leisure

accompagner	to accompany, to go with	les échecs *(m)*	chess
l'activité *(f)*	activity	ensemble	together
aller	to go	envoyer	to send
l'alpinisme *(m)*	mountaineering	l'escalade *(f)*	climbing
s'amuser	to enjoy oneself	faire	to do
l'appel *(m)*	call	faire de l'équitation *Also* faire du cheval	to go horse riding
avoir lieu	to take place	faire de l'exercice	to exercise
la bande dessinée	comic	faire de la voile	to sail
la bicyclette	bicycle	faire des randonnées	to hike
le billet	ticket	faire du bowling	to go bowling
bon marché	cheap	faire du patin à roulettes	to roller-skate
les boules *(f)*	boules	faire du skate	to skateboard
le bowling	bowling	faire partie de	to be a member of
le bureau des objets trouvés	lost property office	fêter	to celebrate
le centre de loisirs	leisure centre	l'histoire d'espionnage *(f)*	spy story
choisir	to choose	l'inconvénient *(m)* *Also* le désavantage	disadvantage
le cinéma	cinema	s'intéresser à	to be interested in
le club	club	le jeu	game
le club des jeunes	youth club	le jeu de cartes	card game
la collection	collection	le jeu de société	board game
collectionner	to collect	le jeu électronique	electronic game
la console de jeux	games console	le jeu vidéo	video game
la danse	dancing	le jouet	toy
danser	to dance	le lecteur DVD	DVD player
débuter	to begin	le lecteur MP3	MP3 player
dessiner	to draw	libre	free (unoccupied)
les distractions *(f)*	things to do	lire	to read
le divertissement	entertainment	le loisir	leisure
donner	to give		

les loisirs	*free-time activities*	se reposer	*to rest*
le magazine Also la revue	*magazine*	retourner	*to go back (somewhere for a second time)*
le membre	*member*		
participer à	*to take part in*	le risque	*risk*
le passe-temps	*pastime, hobby*	le roman policier	*crime novel*
passer du temps	*to spend time*	la salle de jeux	*games room*
la pêche	*fishing*	la séance	*sitting, viewing (e.g. cinema)*
peindre	*to paint*	sortir	*to go out*
le pique-nique	*picnic*	le spectateur	*spectator*
le plaisir	*pleasure*	la surprise-partie	*surprise party*
le portable	*mobile (phone)*	le temps libre	*free time*
promener	*to take for a walk (e.g. dog)*	le terrain de jeux	*play area*
se promener	*to go for a walk*	le texto	*text message*
regarder	*to watch, to look at*	le théâtre	*theatre*
remplir	*to fill*	le vélo	*bike*
se rencontrer	*to meet*	venir	*to come*
rentrer	*to go back (e.g. home)*	voir	*to see*

Higher only:

s'abonner	*to subscribe*	féliciter	*to congratulate*
l'ennui *(m)*	*boredom*	la tournée	*tour, round*
expérimenter	*to experience*	le voilier	*sailing boat*

28

les actualités *(f)*	news	le film de fantaisie	fantasy film
l'affiche *(f)*	poster, notice	le film de guerre	war film
l'annonce *(f)*	advert, notice	le film de science-fiction	science fiction film
l'avantage *(m)*	advantage		
la chaîne	channel (TV), station (radio)	le film policier	detective film
		le film romantique	romantic film, rom com
classique	classical	l'idée *(f)*	idea
la comédie	comedy	les informations *(f)*	news, information
la comédie dramatique	drama	le jeu télévisé	game show
le dessin animé	cartoon	le journal	newspaper
le dictionnaire	dictionary	le journal télévisé	TV news
le documentaire	documentary	la lecture	reading
doublé	dubbed	la pièce de théâtre	play (at the theatre)
l'émission *(f)*	programme		
l'émission jeunesse *(f)*	children's programme	le polar	crime film
		la publicité	advert
l'émission musicale *(f)*	music programme	réel	real
l'émission sportive *(f)*	sports programme	le roman	novel
		la scène	stage
l'exposition *(f)*	exhibition	la série	series
le feuilleton	soap opera	le site	website
le film	film	la téléréalité	reality TV
le film à suspense	thriller	la télévision	television
le film d'action	action film	Also la télé	
le film d'aventure	adventure film	la télévision par câble	cable TV
le film d'épouvante	horror film	la vedette	star, celebrity
le film d'horreur	horror film	le western	western

Higher only:

bref	*brief*	il s'agit de	*it's about*
la comédie de situation	*sitcom*	les sous-titres *(m)*	*subtitles*
les effets spéciaux *(m)*	*special effects*	la télécommande	*remote control*
en différé	*pre-recorded*	la télévision satellite	*satellite TV*
en direct	*live*		

Music

la batterie	*drums*	la musique	*music*
la chaîne hi-fi	*stereo system*	la musique classique	*classical music*
la chanson	*song*	la musique folk	*folk music*
chanter	*to sing*	la musique pop	*pop music*
le chanteur	*singer*	la musique rap	*rap music*
Also la chanteuse		la musique rock	*rock music*
la clarinette	*clarinet*	l'orchestre *(m)*	*orchestra*
le concert	*concert*	le piano	*piano*
le disque compact	*CD*	le saxophone	*saxophone*
le festival de musique	*music festival*	le spectacle	*show*
la flûte	*flute*	la trompette	*trumpet*
la flûte à bec	*recorder*	la version originale	*original version*
le groupe	*group*	le violon	*violin*
la guitare	*guitar*		

Higher only:

la comédie musicale	*musical*	la mélodie	*melody*
les écouteurs *(m)*	*earphones, headphones*		

Personal Information

l'adresse *(f)*	address	moi-même	*myself*
l'adulte *(m/f)*	adult	Monsieur	*Mr*
l'âge *(m)*	age	monsieur	*sir*
aîné	older, first born	mort	*dead*
l'anniversaire *(m)*	birthday	la naissance	*birth*
la carte d'identité	identity card	la nationalité	*nationality*
célèbre	famous	né	*born*
célibataire	single	le nom de jeune fille	*maiden name*
la date de naissance	date of birth	le nom	*surname*
divorcé	divorced	*Also* le nom de famille	
le garçon	boy	le passeport	*passport*
les gens *(m)*	people	pauvre	*poor*
l'homme *(m)*	man	la personne	*person*
l'identité *(f)*	identity	la pièce d'identité	*proof of ID*
jeune	young	porter	*to wear, to carry*
le lieu	place	le prénom	*first name*
le lieu de naissance	place of birth	religieux	*religious*
loger	to stay (in a hotel), to live	riche	*rich*
		sans travail	*unemployed*
Madame	Mrs	signer	*to sign*
madame	madam	le surnom	*nickname*
Mademoiselle	Miss	timide	*shy*
mademoiselle	miss, young lady	tranquille	*quiet*
		vieux	*old*

Higher only:

à la retraite	retired	naître	*to be born*

Personalities

animé	*lively*	impoli	*impolite, rude*
autoritaire	*bossy*	indépendant	*independent*
aventureux	*adventurous*	insupportable	*unbearable*
avoir l'air	*to seem*	intelligent	*intelligent*
bête	*stupid*	négatif	*negative*
le bonheur	*happiness*	la personnalité	*personality*
le caractère	*character, personality*	poli	*polite*
		raisonnable	*reasonable*
charmant	*charming*	rigolo	*funny*
chic	*smart*	sage	*wise, well behaved*
confiant	*confident*		
craintif	*timid, fearful*	sérieux	*serious*
drôle	*funny*	sévère	*strict*
égoïste	*selfish*	silencieux	*silent, quiet*
généreux	*generous*	strict	*strict*
honnête	*honest*	têtu	*stubborn*
impatient	*impatient*		

Higher only:

à l'aise	*at ease*	gâté	*spoilt*
agaçant	*annoying*	jaloux	*jealous*
compréhensif	*understanding*	nerveux	*nervous*
effronté	*cheeky*	prétentieux	*pretentious*
fiable	*reliable*	sensible	*sensitive*
fidèle	*loyal*	sûr de soi	*self-confident*
fier	*proud*	le trait	*trait*
fou	*mad*	vaniteux	*vain*

Relationships

accepter	to accept	éviter	to avoid
adorer	to love	s'excuser	to apologise
agacer	to annoy	expliquer	to explain
aimable	likeable	fâché	angry
l'ami *(m)*	friend (male)	*Also* en colère	
Also le copain		se fâcher	to get angry
amical	friendly	faire la connaissance	to get to know
l'amie *(f)*	friend (female)	la femme	wife
Also la copine		*Also* l'épouse *(f)*	
l'amitié *(f)*	friendship	gentil	kind
l'amour *(m)*	love	s'habituer à	to get used to
apprécier	to appreciate	heureux	happy
attendre	to wait for	la honte	shame
avoir envie de	to fancy	introduire	to introduce
le baiser	kiss	malheureux	unhappy, unlucky
battre	to beat, to hit	le mari	husband
bavard	talkative	*Also* l'époux *(m)*	
bavarder	to chat	le mariage	marriage, wedding
compter sur	to count on	méchant	nasty, fierce
connaître	to know (be familiar with)	les nouvelles *(f)*	news (what someone's been up to)
contribuer	to contribute		
le correspondant	pen friend	oublier	to forget
Also la correspondante		pardonner	to forgive
critiquer	to criticise	le partenaire	partner
discuter	to discuss	*Also* la partenaire	
se disputer	to argue	pénible	awful, painful
divorcer	to divorce	le petit ami	boyfriend
écrire	to write	*Also* le copain	
s'entendre avec	to get on with	la petite amie	girlfriend
s'entendre bien (avec)	to get on well (with)	*Also* la copine	

plaire	to please	respecter	to respect
plaisanter	to joke	rester en contact	to stay in touch
pleurer	to cry	rire	to laugh
présenter	to present	le sens de l'humour	sense of humour
se présenter	to introduce oneself	le sentiment	feeling
		séparé	separated
prêter	to lend	se séparer	to separate
se rappeler	to remember	seul	alone
les rapports *(m)*	relationships	sourire	to smile
refuser	to refuse, to say no	sympa	nice, friendly
remercier	to thank	tchatter	to chat
le rendez-vous	meeting, appointment	la vérité	truth

Higher only:

l'alliance *(f)*	wedding ring	le fiancé *Also* la fiancée	fiancé(e)
cacher	to hide	gêner	to embarrass, to bother, to disturb
le conseil	advice		
coupable	guilty		
déçu	disappointed	humilier	to humiliate
déranger	to disturb	mentir	to lie
la dispute	argument	mépriser	to despise
douter	to doubt	les noces *(f)*	wedding
épouser	to marry	reconnaissant	grateful
exprès	on purpose	tomber amoureux (de)	to fall in love (with)
les fiançailles *(f)*	engagement		

Shopping

acheter	to buy	l'épicerie *(f)*	grocer's
l'argent *(m)*	money	faire des achats	to shop
l'argent de poche *(m)*	pocket money	faire des économies	to save money
avoir besoin de	to need	faire du lèche-vitrines	to go window-shopping
la banque	bank		
la bijouterie	jeweller's	faire les courses	to go shopping (food)
la boucherie	butcher's	faire les magasins	to go shopping (in town)
la boulangerie	baker's	*Also* faire du shopping	
la cabine d'essayage	changing room	la garantie	guarantee
le cadeau	present	garantir	to guarantee
la caisse	till	le grand magasin	department store
la carte bancaire	bank card	gratuit	free (no charge)
la carte de crédit	credit card	le kiosque à journaux	newsstand
cassé	broken	laisser	to leave (an object)
le centre commercial	shopping centre		
la charcuterie	cooked meats shop, delicatessen	la librairie	book shop
		la livraison	delivery
		la livre sterling	pound sterling
le chèque	cheque	le magasin	shop
le choix	choice	*Also* la boutique	
le client	customer	le magasin de chaussures	shoe shop
le coin	corner		
les commerces *(m)*	shops	le magasin d'électroménager	electrical goods shop
coûter	to cost	le magasin de mode	clothes shop
dépenser	to spend	le marchand	market trader
disponible	available	le marché	market
d'occasion	second hand	la marque	brand, make
la droguerie	hardware shop	le mode de paiement	payment method
échanger	to swap, to exchange	la monnaie	change
		neuf	brand new
l'endommagement *(m)*	damage		

le panier	*basket*	le rayon	*department*
la parfumerie	*perfume shop*	le reçu	*receipt*
la pâtisserie	*cake shop*	la réduction	*reduction*
la pièce de remplacement	*replacement part*	réduit	*reduced*
		remplacer	*to replace*
la plainte	*complaint*	la réparation	*repair*
le portefeuille	*wallet*	les soldes *(m)*	*sales*
le porte-monnaie	*purse*	le supermarché	*supermarket*
la poste	*post office*	le tabac	*tobacconist, newsagent*
pousser	*to push*		
le prix	*price*	la valeur	*value*
le produit de remplacement	*replacement product*	vendre	*to sell*
		la vente	*sale*
les provisions *(f)*	*food shopping*	la vitrine	*window*

Higher only:

l'assurance *(f)*	*insurance*	le nettoyage à sec	*dry cleaning*
le commerçant	*shop keeper*	la poissonnerie	*fishmonger's*
la grande surface	*superstore*	le pressing	*dry cleaner's*
l'hypermarché *(m)*	*hypermarket*	la quincaillerie	*ironmonger's*
la laverie automatique	*launderette*	ramener	*to take back*
le libre-service	*self-service*	rapporter	*to take back*
le mode d'emploi	*instructions*	rembourser	*to refund*

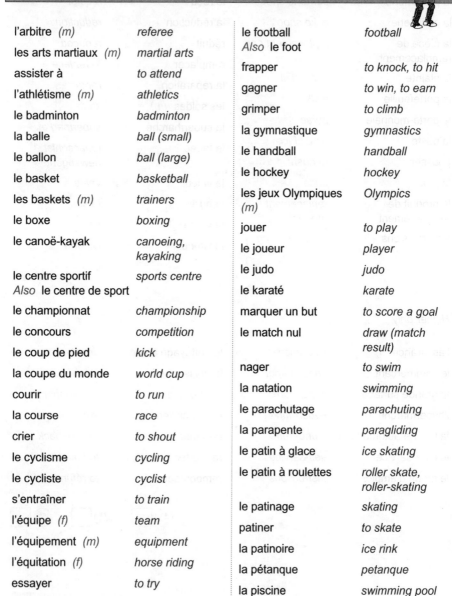

Sport

l'arbitre *(m)*	referee	le football *Also* le foot	football
les arts martiaux *(m)*	martial arts	frapper	to knock, to hit
assister à	to attend	gagner	to win, to earn
l'athlétisme *(m)*	athletics	grimper	to climb
le badminton	badminton	la gymnastique	gymnastics
la balle	ball (small)	le handball	handball
le ballon	ball (large)	le hockey	hockey
le basket	basketball	les jeux Olympiques *(m)*	Olympics
les baskets *(m)*	trainers	jouer	to play
le boxe	boxing	le joueur	player
le canoë-kayak	canoeing, kayaking	le judo	judo
le centre sportif *Also* le centre de sport	sports centre	le karaté	karate
le championnat	championship	marquer un but	to score a goal
le concours	competition	le match nul	draw (match result)
le coup de pied	kick	nager	to swim
la coupe du monde	world cup	la natation	swimming
courir	to run	le parachutage	parachuting
la course	race	la parapente	paragliding
crier	to shout	le patin à glace	ice skating
le cyclisme	cycling	le patin à roulettes	roller skate, roller-skating
le cycliste	cyclist	le patinage	skating
s'entraîner	to train	patiner	to skate
l'équipe *(f)*	team	la patinoire	ice rink
l'équipement *(m)*	equipment	la pétanque	petanque
l'équitation *(f)*	horse riding	la piscine	swimming pool
essayer	to try	la planche à voile	windsurfing
faire de la gymnastique	to do gymnastics		
faire du sport	to do sport		

recevoir	to receive, to be host to
le roller	roller-blading
le rugby	rugby
sauter	to jump
le skate	skateboarding
le ski	skiing
le ski nautique	waterskiing
le sport	sport
sportif	sporty
les sports d'hiver *(m)*	winter sports
les sports extrêmes *(m)*	extreme sports
les sports nautiques *(m)*	water sports
le squash	squash

le stade	stadium
le surf	surfing
surfer	to surf
le tennis	tennis
le tennis de table	table tennis
le terrain	pitch (sports)
toucher	to touch
le trampoline	trampolining
le vestiaire	changing room
la victoire	win, victory
la voile	sailing
le volley	volleyball

Higher only:

les articles de sport *(m)*	sports equipment
l'aviron *(m)*	rowing
la canne à pêche	fishing rod
contrôler	to control, to test
l'entraînement	training
l'escrime *(f)*	fencing
lancer	to throw, to launch
la ligue	league
le maillot de sport	sports shirt, jersey

marquer un essai	to score a try
la mi-temps	half-time, half (of a sports match)
la planche de surf	surf board
la plongée sous-marine	deep-sea diving
la rencontre sportive	sports event
le tir à l'arc	archery
le tournoi	tournament

Technology

l'adresse email *(f)*	email address
à l'attention de	for the attention of
le blog	blog
le bon numéro	correct number
charger	to load
le clavier	keyboard
cliquer	to click
coller	to stick, to paste
contacter	to contact
le cyber harcèlement	cyber bullying
la disquette	disc
l'écran *(m)*	screen
l'électricité *(f)*	electricity
l'email *(m)* *Also* le courrier électronique *Also* le courriel	email
en ligne	online
la façon	way (of doing something)
fonctionner	to work (function)
le forum de discussion	chatroom
l'imprimante *(f)*	printer
imprimer	to print
l'inconvénient *(m)*	disadvantage
lent	slow
le logiciel	software

le message	message
mettre en ligne	to put online
le mot de passe	password
numérique	digital
le numéro de téléphone	phone number
l'ordinateur *(m)*	computer
l'ordinateur portable *(m)*	laptop
l'ordinateur tablette *(m)*	tablet
la page web *Also* la page internet	webpage
le répondeur	answer phone
le réseau social	social network
le site web *Also* le site internet	website
surfer sur internet	to surf the internet
taper	to type
la technologie	technology
télécharger	to download
le téléphone	phone
la toile *Also* le web	internet
la touche	key (of keyboard)
le virus	virus
la webcam	webcam
la Xbox®	Xbox®

Higher only:

appuyer	*to press*	l'icône *(f)*	*icon*
la base de données	*database*	l'internaute *(m)*	*internet user*
le blogueur	*blogger*	le lien	*link*
Also la blogueuse		le moniteur	*monitor*
le bouton	*button*	la page d'accueil	*homepage*
la caméra	*video camera*	la pile	*battery*
le caméscope	*camcorder*	le réseau	*network*
la carte mémoire	*memory card*	sauvegarder	*to back up*
le compte	*account*	le slash	*forward slash*
le disque dur	*hard drive*	le tiret bas	*underscore*
l'écran tactile *(m)*	*touch screen*	le traitement de texte	*word processing*
effacer	*to erase, to rub out*	le webmail	*webmail*
enregistrer	*to record, to save*		

Things to Drink

boire	*to drink*	l'eau minérale *(f)*	*mineral water*
le cacao	*cocoa*	l'eau potable *(f)*	*drinking water*
le café	*café, coffee*	le jus	*juice*
la cafetière	*cafetière*	le jus de fruit	*fruit juice*
le champagne	*champagne*	le lait	*milk*
le chocolat chaud	*hot chocolate*	la limonade	*lemonade*
le cidre	*cider*	la soif	*thirst*
le coca	*coke*	la tasse	*cup*
l'eau *(f)*	*water*	le thé	*tea*

Higher only:

l'infusion *(f)*	*fruit tea*	le lait entier	*full-fat milk*
le lait demi-écrémé	*semi-skimmed milk*	la pression	*draught beer*
le lait écrémé	*skimmed milk*	la soucoupe	*saucer*

Things to Eat

l'agneau *(m)*	*lamb*	le biscuit	*biscuit*
l'alimentation *(f)*	*food*	le bœuf	*beef*
Also la nourriture		les bonbons *(m)*	*sweets*
l'appétit *(m)*	*appetite*	la boulette	*meatball*
la baguette	*French stick, baguette*	la brochette	*kebab*
le beurre	*butter*	le canard	*duck*

les céréales *(f)*	cereal	l'odeur *(f)*	smell
les chips *(m)*	crisps	l'œuf *(m)*	egg
le chocolat	chocolate	l'omelette *(f)*	omelette
la confiture	jam	le pain	bread
la crème	cream	le pâté	pâté
la crêpe	pancake	les pâtes *(f)*	pasta
le croissant	croissant	les pâtisseries *(f)*	pastries
le déjeuner	lunch	le petit déjeuner	breakfast
délicieux	delicious	le petit pain	bread roll
la dinde	turkey	la pizza	pizza
le dîner	dinner, evening meal	le plat cuisiné	ready meal
		la poêle	frying pan
emporter	to take away	le poisson	fish
les escargots *(m)*	snails	le porc	pork
la faim	hunger	la portion	portion
les frites *(f)*	chips	le poulet	chicken
le fromage	cheese	la recette	recipe
les fruits de mer *(m)*	seafood	le repas du soir	evening meal
le gâteau	cake	le riz	rice
la graisse	fat, grease	rôti	roast
le hamburger	hamburger	rôtir	to roast
l'huile *(f)*	oil	le sandwich	sandwich
le jambon	ham	la sauce vinaigrette	salad dressing
la liste	list	la saucisse	sausage
manger	to eat	le saucisson	sausage (like salami)
la margarine	margarine		
mélangé	mixed	le saumon	salmon
mélanger	to mix	savoureux	tasty
le miel	honey	la soupe	soup
les moules *(f)*	mussels	*Also* le potage	
la moutarde	mustard	les spaghettis *(m)*	spaghetti
nourrir	to feed		

le steak	steak	le thon	tuna
Also le bifteck		la truite	trout
le steak haché	burger	la vanille	vanilla
le sucre	sugar	la viande	meat
sucré	sweet	la viande hachée	mince
la tarte	tart, pie	le vinaigre	vinegar
la tartine	(slice of) bread and butter	le yaourt	yoghurt

Higher only:

à la vapeur	steamed	goûteux	tasty
amer	bitter	la noix	nut
la casserole	saucepan	les nouilles (f)	noodles
cru	raw	l'œuf à la coque (m)	boiled egg
les cuisses de grenouille (f)	frogs' legs	Also l'œuf dur (m)	
		l'œuf au plat (m)	fried egg
dégoûtant	disgusting	l'œuf brouillé (m)	scrambled egg
fait maison	home-made	l'oie (f)	goose
la farine	flour	le pâté de foie gras	goose liver pâté
le foie	liver	la pistache	pistachio
le fromage de chèvre	goat's cheese	le souper	supper
fumé	smoked	le veau	veal

Accommodation

l'accueil *(m)*	welcome (desk)	le gîte	holiday cottage
l'ascenseur *(m)*	lift	l'hôtel *(m)*	hotel
l'auberge de jeunesse *(f)*	youth hostel	le lavabo	basin, washbasin
		le logement	accommodation
le bain	bath	le loyer	rent
le balcon	balcony	la pension complète	full board
la chambre	room	la piscine couverte	indoor swimming pool
la chambre à deux lits	twin room		
la chambre de famille	family room	recommander	to recommend
la chambre double	double room	la réservation	reservation, booking
la chambre pour deux personnes	double room		
		réserver	to reserve
la chambre pour une personne	single room	le sac de couchage	sleeping bag
		la salle de bain	bathroom
confirmer	to confirm	le savon	soap
le confort	comfort	la sortie	way out, exit
de luxe	luxury	la sortie de secours	emergency exit
la demi-pension	half-board	le tarif	rate
le dortoir	dormitory	le tarif réduit	reduced rate
la douche	shower	la tente	tent
l'entrée *(f)*	entrance	la vue	view
l'étoile *(f)*	star	la vue sur la mer	sea view
faire du camping	to go camping		

Higher only:

accueillir	to welcome	dresser une tente	to pitch a tent
la chambre d'hôte	bed and breakfast	héberger	to lodge
		prière de	please (request)

Buildings

l'appartement *(m)*	flat, apartment	l'immeuble *(m)*	building (usually high-rise)
le bâtiment	building	la maison	house
la cathédrale	cathedral	la maison des jeunes	youth club
la cave	cellar	la maison individuelle	detached house
le chauffage central	central heating	la maison jumelée	semi-detached house
la clé	key		
Also la clef		la maison mitoyenne	terraced house
la climatisation	air conditioning	la mosquée	mosque
Also la clim		le mur	wall
le commissariat	police station	le musée	museum
le couloir	corridor	la pièce	room
dehors	outside	la porte	door
descendre	to go down	la porte d'entrée	front door
l'église *(f)*	church	privé	private
entrer	to enter	la réception	reception
l'escalier *(m)*	staircase	le rez-de-chaussée	ground floor
l'étage *(m)*	floor (of a building)	la salle	room, hall
la fenêtre	window	le sous-sol	basement
fermé à clef	locked	spacieux	spacious
le grenier	attic	les toilettes *(f)*	toilets
historique	historic	le vestiaire	cloakroom
l'hôtel de ville *(m)*	town hall		
Also la mairie			

Higher only:

la caisse d'épargne	savings bank	la gendarmerie	police station
donner sur	to look out over	la maison de retraite	retirement house
l'échelle *(f)*	ladder	le vestibule	foyer
l'étagère *(f)*	shelf		

City, Town and Village

l'ambiance *(f)*	atmosphere	interdit	forbidden
ancien	ancient, former	*Also* défendu	
l'arrêt d'autobus *(m)*	bus stop	le jardin public	park
la banlieue	suburb	multiculturel	multicultural
la bibliothèque	library	municipal	public, municipal
le bruit	noise	le niveau	level
le bureau	office	le palais	palace
calme	quiet	le panneau	sign
la campagne	country(side)	le parking	car park
le centre-ville	town centre	le passage piéton	pedestrian crossing
le code postal	postcode	perdu	lost
l'espace *(m)*	space	la place	square
la ferme	farm	le pont	bridge
la fermeture	closure	public	public
la fête	holiday, festival, party	le quartier	district
la foule	crowd	la route	road
la grande rue	main street	la station de métro	underground station
l'habitant *(m)*	inhabitant	le taxi	taxi
habiter	to live	le trottoir	pavement
l'industrie *(f)*	industry	se trouver	to be located
industriel	industrial	le village	village
		la ville	town

Higher only:

l'arrondissement *(m)*	borough, district	la fontaine	fountain
le cambriolage	burglary	paraître	to appear
le canal	canal	le passage à niveau	level crossing
le distributeur d'argent	cash point	remarquer	to remark, to notice
entouré	surrounded		
les environs *(m)*	surrounding area		

Environment

la boîte en carton	carton	le pétrole	oil (from the ground)
bruyant	noisy	la piste cyclable	cycle path
le centre de recyclage	recycling point	la planète	planet
le charbon	coal	pollué	polluted
la circulation	traffic	polluer	to pollute
cultiver	to grow (plants)	la pollution	pollution
les déchets *(m)*	rubbish	la poubelle	rubbish bin
le désastre	disaster	le problème	problem
Also la catastrophe		propre	clean
détruire	to destroy	la protection	protection
disparaître	to disappear	protéger	to protect
économiser	to save	le réchauffement climatique	global warming
l'embouteillage *(m)*	traffic jam	*Also* le réchauffement de la terre	
en danger	in danger		
l'endroit *(m)*	place	recyclable	recyclable
l'énergie *(f)*	energy	recycler	to recycle
l'environnement *(m)*	environment	réduire	to reduce
l'espace vert *(m)*	green space	les ressources naturelles *(f)*	natural resources
faire du recyclage	to recycle	le sac plastique	plastic bag
fournir	to provide	sale	dirty
gaspiller	to waste	sans plomb	unleaded
le gaz	gas	sauver	to save
international	international	les transports en commun *(m)*	public transport
jeter	to throw		
manque de	lack of	utiliser	to use
mondial	global	la zone piétonne	pedestrian zone
l'ouragan *(m)*	hurricane		

Higher only:

abîmer	*to damage, to spoil*	l'énergie solaire *(f)*	*solar power*
améliorer	*to improve*	l'espèce *(f)*	*species*
augmenter	*to increase*	faire du compost	*to make compost*
l'avertissement *(m)*	*warning*	fondre	*to melt*
bénéficier	*to benefit*	le gaz carbonique	*carbon dioxide, carbon monoxide*
climatique	*climate*	le gaz d'échappement	*exhaust fumes*
la consommation	*consumption*	l'incendie *(m)*	*fire (emergency)*
construire	*to build*	la lumière	*light*
contaminer	*to contaminate*	les ordures *(f)*	*waste*
la couche d'ozone	*ozone layer*	la paix	*peace*
le déboisement	*deforestation*	la perte	*loss, waste*
les dégâts *(m)*	*damage*	produire	*to produce*
l'eau douce *(f)*	*fresh water*	ramasser	*to collect, to gather*
l'eau salée *(f)*	*salt water*	renouvelable	*renewable*
l'effet de serre *(m)*	*greenhouse effect*	surpeuplé	*overpopulated*
l'emballage *(m)*	*packaging*	le tremblement de terre	*earthquake*
endommager	*to damage, to harm*	trier	*to sort*
l'énergie renouvelable *(f)*	*renewable energy*	le volcan	*volcano*

Furniture

l'armoire *(f)*	*wardrobe*	le miroir	*mirror*
la chaise	*chair*	le placard	*cupboard*
le fauteuil	*armchair*	le rideau	*curtain*
le lit	*bed*	la table	*table*
le meuble	*piece of furniture*	le téléphone	*telephone*

Higher only:

l'horloge *(f)*	*clock*	meublé	*furnished*
Also la pendule		le tiroir	*drawer*
les lits superposés *(m)*	*bunk beds*		

Health

actif	*active*	avoir mal au ventre	*to have a tummy ache*
aider	*to help*		
aller bien	*to be well*	se blesser	*to get injured*
aller mieux	*to be better*	casser	*to break*
arrêter de	*to stop (doing something)*	la cigarette	*cigarette*
Also cesser de		le comprimé	*tablet*
s'arrêter	*to stop (moving)*	le coup de soleil	*sunburn, sun stroke*
l'aspirine *(f)*	*aspirin*		
avoir mal à la gorge	*to have a sore throat*	la crème solaire	*sun cream*
		dangereux	*dangerous*
avoir mal à la tête	*to have a headache*	se détendre	*to relax*
		Also se relaxer	

la drogue	*drug(s)*	le médicament	*medicine*
se droguer	*to take drugs*	mourir	*to die*
en bonne santé	*in good health*	le non fumeur	*non-smoker*
en forme	*fit*	l'obésité *(f)*	*obesity*
équilibré	*balanced*	ordinaire	*ordinary, everyday*
faire de la musculation	*to do weight training*	paresseux	*lazy*
se faire mal	*to injure yourself*	la peur	*fear*
fatigant	*tiring*	la pilule	*pill*
fatigué	*tired*	prendre	*to take*
la fièvre	*temperature, fever*	le régime	*diet*
		rester	*to stay*
fort	*strong*	le rhume	*cold*
frais	*cool*	sain	*healthy*
fumer	*to smoke*	salé	*savoury, salty*
le fumeur	*smoker*	la santé	*health*
goûter	*to taste*	sentir	*to smell, to feel*
gras	*fatty*	se sentir	*to feel*
gratter	*to scratch*	le sommeil	*sleep*
la grippe	*flu*	tomber	*to fall*
grossir	*to put on weight*	tousser	*to cough*
le gymnase	*gym, gymnasium*	tuer	*to kill*
l'habitude *(f)*	*habit*	végétarien	*vegetarian*
l'hôpital *(m)*	*hospital*	vérifier	*to check*
s'inquiéter	*to worry*	vide	*empty*
maigrir	*to lose weight*	la vitamine	*vitamin*
malade	*ill*	vivre	*to live*
la maladie	*illness*	vomir	*to vomit, to be sick*
malsain	*unhealthy*		

Higher only:

accro	*addicted*	gâcher	*to spoil*
alcoolique	*alcoholic (person)*	hors d'haleine	*out of breath*
		ivre	*drunk*
alcoolisé	*alcoholic (drink)*	la matière grasse	*fat (in food)*
l'alcoolisme *(m)*	*alcoholism*	mener	*to lead*
avertir	*to warn*	la nourriture bio	*organic food*
le cancer des poumons	*lung cancer*	la piqûre	*injection*
crevé	*exhausted, tired*	renoncer	*to give up*
la crise cardiaque	*heart attack*	respirer	*to breathe*
déprimé	*depressed*	le sida	*AIDS*
désintoxiquer	*to detox*	soigner	*to treat, to care for*
la douleur	*pain*		
s'enivrer	*to get drunk*	le soin	*care*
épuiser	*to exhaust*	le tabagisme	*smoking*
s'entraîner	*to train, to practise*	le toxicomane	*drug addict*
		Also la toxicomane	
essoufflé	*breathless*		

Holidays and Festivals

l'appareil photo *(m)*	camera	le Jour de l'An	New Year's Day
se baigner	to go bathing, to go for a swim	le jour férié	public holiday
		la langue	language
le bloc sanitaire	shower block	le lundi de Pâques	Easter Monday
le bord de la mer	seaside	la mer	sea
bronzer	to sunbathe, to go brown	Noël	Christmas
le camping	campsite	le Nouvel An	New Year
le Carême	Lent	offrir	to give (presents)
la carte postale	postcard	Pâques	Easter
la chambre d'hôte	guest room	le parc d'attractions	theme park
la colonie de vacances	summer camp, holiday camp	la plage	beach
		le poisson d'avril	April Fools' Day
la côte	coast	la promenade	walk
l'emplacement *(m)*	pitch (for a tent)	la randonnée	hike
en plein air	outside	le sable	sand
faire une promenade	to go for a walk	la Saint-Sylvestre	New Year's Eve
la fête des mères	Mother's day	la Saint-Valentin	Valentine's Day
la fête des Rois	Epiphany	le terrain de camping	camping pitch
la fête du travail	May Day	les vacances *(f)*	holiday(s)
les feux d'artifice *(m)*	fireworks	les vacances d'hiver *(f)*	winter holidays
les grandes vacances	summer holidays	la veille de Noël	Christmas Eve
le jour de congé	day off (holiday)	le vendredi saint	Good Friday

Higher only:

le défilé	procession, parade	le spectacle son et lumière	sound and light show
la messe	mass	les vacances de neige *(f)*	winter holiday
la Pentecôte	Pentecost		

In the Home

allumer	to light, to turn on	la lampe	lamp
l'aspirateur (m)	hoover	laver la voiture	to wash the car
commode	convenient, handy	le lave-vaisselle	dishwasher
confortable	comfortable	le linge de lit	bed linen
le congélateur	freezer	la machine à laver	washing machine
la cuisine	kitchen	mettre	to put
la cuisinière	cooker	montrer	to show
déménager	to move house	la nappe	tablecloth
le domicile	home	nettoyer	to clean
le drap	sheet	l'oreiller (m)	pillow
en désordre	untidy	l'outil (m)	tool
s'endormir	to go to sleep	le papier hygiénique	toilet paper
faire du baby-sitting	to babysit	passer l'aspirateur	to do the hoovering
faire du jardinage	to do the gardening	rangé	tidy
faire la vaisselle	to do the washing up	ranger	to tidy
		renverser	to knock over
faire le lit	to make the bed	réparer	to repair
faire le ménage	to do the housework	repasser	to iron
		le robinet	tap
le four	oven	la salle à manger	dining room
le four à micro-ondes Also le micro-ondes	microwave	la salle de séjour	living room
		le salon	lounge
le frigo	fridge	le sofa	sofa
le garage	garage	le tableau	picture, board
garder	to keep, to look after	le téléviseur	television (set)
l'image (f)	picture	tirer	to pull

Higher only:

le bricolage	*DIY*
le cabinet de travail	*study*
couvrir	*to cover*

éteindre	*to turn off (the lights)*
le foyer	*home*
la moquette	*carpet*

Location and Distance

à droite	*on the right*	là-bas	*over there*
à gauche	*on the left*	loin	*far (away)*
à l'extérieur	*outside*	le milieu	*middle*
à l'intérieur	*inside*	le nord	*north*
chez	*at (someone's house)*	nulle part	*nowhere*
		l'ouest *(m)*	*west*
continuez	*continue*	par	*through*
de chaque côté	*on each side*	partout	*everywhere*
la direction	*direction*	proche	*close*
en bas	*below, underneath*	quelque part	*somewhere*
		situé	*situated*
en haut	*above*	le sud	*south*
l'est *(m)*	*east*	tournez à droite	*turn right*
ici	*here*	tournez à gauche	*turn left*
inférieur	*lower, inferior*	tout droit	*straight on*
intérieur	*inside, inner, internal*	tout près	*really near*
le kilomètre	*kilometre*	toutes directions	*all directions, all traffic*
là	*there*		

Higher only:

là-haut	*up there*

Nature

agricole	*agricultural*	le lac	*lake*
l'arbre *(m)*	*tree*	la lune	*moon*
le champ	*field*	la montagne	*mountain*
le chemin	*path, way*	la nature	*nature*
la colline	*hill*	l'océan *(m)*	*ocean*
le feu	*fire*	le parc	*park*
la fleur	*flower*	la pelouse	*lawn, grass*
le fleuve	*river (that flows into the sea)*	pittoresque	*picturesque*
		la plante	*plant*
la forêt	*forest*	la rivière	*river (that flows into another river)*
l'île *(f)*	*island*		
l'inondation *(f)*	*flood*		
le jardin	*garden*	la terre	*earth, ground*
le jardin publique	*public gardens, park*		

Higher only:

l'espèce *(f)*	*species, sort, kind*	le paysage	*countryside*
		le sommet	*summit*
l'herbe *(f)*	*grass*	la vague	*wave*
inonder	*to flood*	le zoo	*zoo*
la marée	*tide*	*Also* le jardin zoologique	

Places

à l'étranger	*abroad*
africain	*African*
l'Afrique *(f)*	*Africa*
l'Algérie *(f)*	*Algeria*
algérien	*Algerian*
l'Allemagne *(f)*	*Germany*
allemand	*German*
les Alpes *(f)*	*Alps*
américain	*American*
l'Amérique *(f)*	*America*
l'Amérique du Nord *(f)*	*North America*
l'Amérique du Sud *(f)*	*South America*
anglais	*English*
l'Angleterre *(f)*	*England*
l'Asie *(f)*	*Asia*
l'Atlantique *(m)*	*Atlantic Ocean*
l'Australie *(f)*	*Australia*
l'Autriche *(f)*	*Austria*
autrichien	*Austrian*
belge	*Belgian*
la Belgique	*Belgium*
la Bourgogne	*Burgundy*
la Bretagne	*Brittany*
britannique	*British*
le Canada	*Canada*
canadien	*Canadian*
la Chine	*China*
chinois	*Chinese*
la Corse	*Corsica*
corse	*Corsican*

le Danemark	*Denmark*
danois	*Danish*
le département	*administrative district, county*
Douvres	*Dover*
le drapeau	*flag*
écossais	*Scottish*
l'Écosse *(f)*	*Scotland*
Édimbourg	*Edinburgh*
l'Espagne *(f)*	*Spain*
espagnol	*Spanish*
les États-Unis *(m)*	*United States*
l'Europe *(f)*	*Europe*
européen	*European*
la France	*France*
gallois	*Welsh*
la Grande-Bretagne	*Great Britain*
grec	*Greek*
la Grèce	*Greece*
la Guyane	*French Guiana*
hollandais	*Dutch*
la Hollande	*Holland*
l'Inde *(f)*	*India*
indien	*Indian*
irlandais	*Irish*
l'Irlande *(f)*	*Ireland*
l'Irlande du Nord *(f)*	*Northern Ireland*
l'Italie *(f)*	*Italy*
italien	*Italian*
le Japon	*Japan*

japonais	*Japanese*	polonais	*Polish*
Londres	*London*	portugais	*Portuguese*
la Manche	*English Channel*	le Portugal	*Portugal*
le Maroc	*Morocco*	la province	*province*
marocain	*Moroccan*	les Pyrénées *(f)*	*Pyrenees*
le Massif Central	*Central France*	la région	*region*
la Méditerranée	*Mediterranean*	la Réunion	*Réunion*
le Midi	*south of France*	le Royaume-Uni	*United Kingdom*
le monde	*world*	russe	*Russian*
la Normandie	*Normandy*	la Russie	*Russia*
le Pakistan	*Pakistan*	le Sénégal	*Senegal*
pakistanais	*Pakistani*	la Suisse	*Switzerland*
le pays	*country*	suisse	*Swiss*
le Pays de Galles	*Wales*	la Tunisie	*Tunisia*
le Pays-Bas	*Netherlands*	tunisien	*Tunisian*
la Picardie	*Picardy*	turc	*Turkish*
la Pologne	*Poland*	la Turquie	*Turkey*

Social Issues

l'ado *(m/f)* *Also* l'adolescent *(m)*	*teenager, young person*	combattre	*to combat*
âgé	*old, aged*	le commerce équitable	*fair trade*
l'association caritative *(f)* *Also* l'organisation charitable *(f)*	*charity*	se comporter	*to behave*
		le dommage	*pity, shame*
		l'égalité *(f)*	*equality*
attaquer	*to attack*	l'état *(m)*	*state*
avoir peur	*to be afraid*	la famine	*famine*

la grève	*strike*	la priorité	*priority*
la guerre	*war*	la réduction	*reduction*
il faut	*you have to, it is necessary to*	la reine	*queen*
		responsable	*responsible*
important	*important*	le roi	*king*
impossible	*impossible*	sans-abri	*homeless*
inclus	*included*	la sécheresse	*drought*
injuste	*unfair*	la sécurité	*security*
l'instruction civique *(f)*	*citizenship*	le sondage	*opinion poll, survey*
la jeunesse	*youth*		
obliger	*to oblige, to force*	le taux	*rate*
l'organisation caritative *(f)*	*charity*	tout le monde	*everybody*
		typique	*typical*
la pauvreté	*poverty*	l'urgence *(f)*	*emergency*
les personnes défavorisées *(f)*	*underprivileged people*	le vandalisme	*vandalism*
		le vol	*theft*
le Premier Ministre	*Prime Minister*	voler	*to steal*
prévenir	*to avoid, to prevent, to warn*	le voleur	*thief*

Higher only:

affamé	*starving*	les droits de l'homme *(m)*	*human rights*
agresser	*to mug*		
l'attaque *(f)*	*attack*	effrayant	*scary, frightening*
au profit de	*in aid of*	égal	*equal*
la bande	*gang*	l'enquête *(f)*	*inquiry, inquest*
la bonne action	*good deed*	envahir	*to invade*
déchirer	*to tear*	l'espionnage *(m)*	*spying*
désavantager	*to disadvantage*	les exclus *(m)*	*outcasts, socially excluded people*
la dette	*debt*		
la discrimination	*discrimination*	le harcèlement	*harassment*

harceler	*to harass*	réfléchir	*to think, to reflect*
illégal	*illegal*	le réfugié	*refugee*
l'immigré *(m)*	*immigrant*	la retraite	*retirement*
les incivilités *(f)*	*antisocial behaviour*	sexiste	*sexist*
		soutenir	*to support*
inconnu	*unknown*	supprimer	*to eliminate*
s'inquiéter	*to worry*	survivre	*to survive*
la loi	*law*	le témoin	*witness*
lutter	*to struggle*	tenter	*to attempt*
mal nourri	*malnourished*	le travail volontaire	*voluntary work*
la manifestation	*demonstration, protest*	le troisième âge	*old age*
menacer	*to threaten*	valoir mieux	*to be better*
le mineur	*underage person*	la vente de charité	*charity sale*
les produits bio *(m)*	*organic products*	la victime	*victim*
le racisme	*racism*	le volontaire	*volunteer*
raciste	*racist*	le voyou	*delinquent, yob*
réaliser	*to realise*		

😌☐   😃☐   😊☐

Tourism

à l'étranger	*abroad*
l'aire de jeux *(f)*	*play area*
l'aventure *(f)*	*adventure*
la brochure	*brochure*
le bureau des renseignements	*information office*
le château	*castle*
chercher	*to look for*
commercial	*commercial*
s'échapper	*to escape*
l'étranger *(m)*	*foreigner, stranger*
l'euro *(m)*	*euro*
l'excursion *(f)*	*trip*
fermé	*closed*
la frontière	*border*
la galerie d'art	*art gallery*
la liste des prix	*price list*
le monument	*monument*

l'office de tourisme *(m)* Also le syndicat d'initiative	*tourist information office*
le plan de ville Also le plan de la ville	*map of the town*
les renseignements *(m)*	*information*
le séjour	*stay*
le site touristique Also l'attraction *(f)*	*tourist attraction*
le souvenir	*souvenir*
la station de ski	*ski resort*
le tour	*tour*
le tourisme	*tourism*
le touriste Also la touriste	*tourist*
touristique	*tourist (adjective)*
la visite	*visit, tour*
la visite guidée	*guided tour*
visiter	*to visit*

Higher only:

le contrôle de passeport	*passport control*
l'enregistrement *(m)*	*check-in*
la foire	*fair*
l'hospitalité *(f)*	*hospitality*
jumelé	*twinned*

la location de vélos	*bike hire*
séjourner	*to stay*
la station balnéaire	*seaside resort*
le taux de change	*exchange rate*
le voyage organisé	*package holiday*

Transport

à pied	on foot	la ligne	line, route
aller à pied	to walk	marcher	to walk
l'aller-retour *(m)*	return	le métro	metro, underground
l'aller-simple *(m)*	single	la mobylette	moped
l'arrivée *(f)*	arrival	monter	to climb, to get on
l'autobus *(m)*	bus		
l'autoroute *(f)*	motorway	la moto	motorbike
l'avion *(m)*	plane	le moyen de transport	means of transport
le bateau	boat		
le camion	lorry	le navire	ship
le car	coach	la panne	breakdown
le carrefour	crossroads	le permis	licence
la carte routière	road map	le permis de conduire	driving licence
le chemin de fer	railway	le piéton	pedestrian
composter	to validate (a ticket)	le poids lourd	heavy-goods (vehicle)
le conducteur	driver	le quai	platform
conduire	to drive	rapide	fast
le délai	time period	le retour	return (journey)
le départ	departure	le rond-point	roundabout
l'essence *(f)*	petrol	rouler	to go along (in a car)
l'essence sans plomb *(f)*	unleaded petrol		
le ferry	ferry	la rue	street
les feux *(m)*	traffic lights	sens interdit	no entry
la gare	station	sens unique	one way
la gare routière	coach station	stationner *Also* se garer	to park
le gasoil	diesel		
le guichet	ticket office	suivre	to follow
l'horaire *(m)*	timetable	tourner	to turn
lentement	slowly	le train	train

le tramway	*tram*	la vitesse	*speed, gear*
les transports en commun *(m)*	*public transport*	la voiture *Also* l'auto *(f)*	*car*
le véhicule	*vehicle*	vous allez à pied?	*are you going on foot?*

Higher only:

la ceinture de sécurité	*seatbelt*	l'hélicoptère *(m)*	*helicopter*
diriger	*to direct*	l'intersection *(f)*	*junction*
doubler	*to overtake*	la limitation de vitesse	*speed limit*
écraser	*to run over*	les phares *(m)*	*headlights*
l'express *(m)*	*fast train*	ralentir	*to slow down*
le frein	*brake*	stationnement interdit	*no parking*
freiner	*to brake*	le transport aérien	*air transport*

Travel

l'aéroport *(m)*	*airport*	le contrôle des passeports	*passport control*
l'agence de voyages *(f)*	*travel agency*	le contrôleur	*ticket inspector*
attacher	*to attach*	la correspondance	*connection*
les bagages *(m)*	*luggage*	défaire la valise	*to unpack a suitcase*
le buffet	*snack bar*	descendre de	*to get out of*
la caravane	*caravan*	la destination	*destination*
le carnet	*book of tickets*	direct	*direct*
la classe	*class*	la douane	*customs*
le compartiment	*compartment*	l'étape *(f)*	*stage (of a journey)*
la consigne	*left luggage*		

faire la valise	*to pack a suitcase*	revenir	*to come back*
la location	*rental, hire*	le sac à dos	*rucksack, backpack*
la location de voiture	*car rental, car hire*	la salle d'attente	*waiting room*
louer	*to rent, to hire*	la station service	*service station*
se mettre en route	*to take to the road, to get going*	se terminer	*to end*
		le trajet	*journey*
monter dans	*to get into*	la traversée	*crossing*
partir	*to leave, to go*	traverser	*to cross*
le passager	*passenger*	valable	*valid*
le péage	*toll, tollbooth*	la valise	*suitcase*
le port	*port*	le vol	*flight*
prêt	*ready*	le voyage	*journey*
quitter	*to leave (a place)*	*Also* le trajet	
rater	*to miss (e.g. train)*	voyager	*to travel*
		le voyageur	*traveller*
		le wagon-lit	*sleeping car*

Higher only:

atterrir	*to land*	manquer	*to miss*
la croisière	*cruise*	la portière	*door*
décoller	*to take off*	traduire	*to translate*
embarquer	*to board*	le Tunnel sous la Manche	*Channel Tunnel*
en provenance de	*coming from*		
l'heure de pointe *(f)*	*rush hour*		

☹ ☐   ☺ ☐   ☺ ☐

Weather

l'averse *(f)*	*shower*	la brume	*mist*
briller	*to shine*	la chaleur	*heat*
le brouillard	*fog*	chaud	*hot*

le ciel	sky	le nuage	cloud
le climat	climate	nuageux	cloudy
couvert	overcast	l'ombre (f)	shadow, shade
le degré	degree	l'orage (m)	storm (thunder)
doux	mild, soft	orageux	stormy
l'éclair (m)	lightning	pleuvoir	to rain
l'éclaircie (f)	sunny interval	la pluie	rain
ensoleillé	sunny	pluvieux	rainy
faire beau	to be nice weather	les prévisions météo (f)	weather forecast
faire mauvais	to be bad weather	sec	dry
		le soleil	sun
froid	cold	la température	temperature
geler	to freeze	la température maximale	highest temperature
la glace	ice	la température minimale	lowest temperature
humide	wet, damp		
il y a des éclairs	there's lightning	la tempête	storm (wind)
la météo	weather forecast	le temps	time, weather
mouillé	wet	le tonnerre	thunder
la neige	snow	tremper	to soak
neiger	to snow	le vent	wind

Higher only:

brumeux	misty	la température élevée	high temperature
s'éclaircir	to brighten up	la température moyenne	average temperature
la grêle	hail	tiède	tepid, lukewarm
grêler	to hail	variable	changeable
incertain	uncertain		
la température basse	low temperature		

Future Plans

l'ambition *(f)*	ambition	expérimenté	experienced
l'année sabbatique *(f)*	gap year	faire des études	to study
l'avenir *(m)*	future	mériter	to deserve
avoir l'intention de	to intend to	mettre de l'argent de côté	to save money
bien payé	well paid	l'occasion *(f)*	opportunity
le cauchemar	nightmare	prévu	foreseen, planned
certainement	certainly		
le certificat	certificate	le projet	plan, project
le conseiller d'orientation	careers adviser	les projets pour l'avenir *(m)*	future plans
craindre	to fear	le rêve	dream
décider	to decide	rêver	to dream
devenir	to become	souhaiter	to wish
le diplôme	qualification	l'université *(f)*	university
l'entrevue *(f)*	interview		

Higher only:

assurer	to assure, to insure	l'établissement *(m)*	establishment
la confiance	confidence	les études universitaires *(f)*	higher education
conseiller	to advise	la faculté	faculty, university
le débouché	prospect	former	to train
élargir	to widen	la licence	degree (university)
empêcher	to prevent		
l'enseignement *(m)*	teaching	la médecine	medicine
l'espoir *(m)*	hope	le souci	worry

Jobs

l'acteur *(m)*	actor	la factrice	postwoman
l'actrice *(f)*	actress	faire du baby-sitting	to babysit
l'agent de police *(m)*	police officer	le fermier	farmer
l'agriculteur *(m)*	farmer	Also la fermière	
l'architecte *(m)*	architect	le fonctionnaire	civil servant
Also l'architecte *(f)*		Also la fonctionnaire	
l'artiste *(m)*	artist	l'homme d'affaires *(m)*	businessman
le boucher	butcher	l'hôtesse de l'air *(f)*	air hostess
Also la bouchère		l'infirmier *(m)*	nurse
le boulanger	baker	Also l'infirmière *(f)*	
Also la boulangère		l'informaticien *(m)*	computer
le caissier	cashier, checkout	Also l'informaticienne *(f)*	scientist
Also la caissière	assistant	l'ingénieur *(m)*	engineer
le chauffeur	driver (e.g. of a taxi)	le journaliste	journalist
		Also la journaliste	
le coiffeur	hairdresser	le maçon	builder
Also la coiffeuse		le maître	teacher (primary
le concierge	caretaker	Also la maîtresse	school only)
Also la concierge		le mécanicien	mechanic
le cuisinier	cook	Also la mécanicienne	
Also la cuisinière		le médecin	doctor (medical)
le dentiste	dentist	le musicien	musician
Also la dentiste		Also la musicienne	
le dessinateur	designer	le petit job	part-time job
le docteur	doctor (non-medical)	le pharmacien	pharmacist
l'électricien *(m)*	electrician	Also la pharmacienne	
Also l'électricienne *(f)*		le plombier	plumber
l'emploi *(m)*	job	le poète	poet
l'enseignant *(m)*	teacher	le policier	policeman
Also l'enseignante *(f)*		Also le gendarme	
l'épicier *(m)*	grocer	la policière	policewoman
Also l'épicière *(f)*		Also la gendarme	
le facteur	postman		

le pompier	*fireman*	le steward	*air steward*
le programmeur	*programmer*	le technicien	*technician*
le réceptionniste	*receptionist*	*Also* la technicienne	
le représentant	*rep(resentative)*	le vendeur	*salesman,*
Also la représentante		*Also* la vendeuse	*saleswoman*
le secrétaire	*secretary*	le vétérinaire	*vet*
Also la secrétaire		*Also* la vétérinaire	
le serveur	*waiter, waitress*		
Also la serveuse			

Higher only:

l'auteur *(m)*	*author*	l'interprète *(m)*	*interpreter*
l'avocat *(m)*	*lawyer, barrister*	*Also* l'interprète *(f)*	
Also l'avocate *(f)*		le jardinier	*gardener*
le comptable	*accountant*	*Also* la jardinière	
Also la comptable		le mannequin	*model*
le dessinateur de mode	*fashion designer*	l'ouvrier *(m)*	*worker*
l'écrivain *(m)*	*writer*	*Also* l'ouvrière *(f)*	
le fleuriste	*florist*	le prêtre	*priest*
Also la fleuriste		*Also* le curé	

School Equipment

les affaires *(f)*	things, items	la gomme	rubber
le bloc-notes	pad of paper	le livre	book
le cahier	exercise book	le livre d'école	school book
la calculette	calculator	la page	page
Also la calculatrice		le projecteur	projector
le cartable	schoolbag	le pupitre	desk
les ciseaux *(m)*	scissors	la règle	rule, ruler
la colle	glue	le stylo	pen
le crayon	pencil	le stylo à encre	fountain pen
le feutre	felt tip	le taille-crayon	sharpener
la fiche de travail	worksheet	la trousse	pencil case

Higher only:

bien équipé	well equipped	mal équipé	ill equipped
la cartouche d'encre	ink cartridge	le stylo bille	ballpoint pen

School Life

l'année scolaire *(f)*	school year	encourager	to encourage
le bac	school leaving exams, A-levels	les études *(f)*	studies
		l'étudiant *(m)*	student
le baccalauréat	A-levels	étudier	to study
le brevet	GCSE	l'examen *(m)*	exam(ination)
calculer	to calculate	l'excursion scolaire *(f)*	school trip
le certificat de fin d'études	school leaving certificate	l'exemple *(m)*	example
		l'exercice *(m)*	exercise
la chorale	choir	l'expérience *(f)*	experiment
comprendre	to understand	se faire des amis	to make friends
copier	to copy	le groupe scolaire	school group
le cours *Also* la leçon	lesson	le groupe théâtral	drama group
		l'instituteur *(m)* *Also* l'institutrice *(f)*	primary teacher
demander	to ask		
le détail	detail	la journée scolaire	school day
la difficulté	difficulty	laisser tomber	to drop
le directeur *Also* la directrice	head teacher, director	la liberté	freedom
		le mi-trimestre	half-term
distribuer	to distribute, to give out	mixte	mixed
		la note	grade
le droit	right	oral	oral
l'échange *(m)*	exchange	parler	to speak
éducatif	educational	passer un examen	to sit an exam
l'éducation *(f)*	education	la pause *Also* la récréation	break
l'élève *(m/f)*	pupil		
l'emploi du temps *(m)*	timetable	perdre	to lose
en première	in year 12, in lower sixth	poser	to put
		pouvoir	to be able to
en seconde	in year 11	pratiquer	to practise
en sixième	in year 7	préparer	to prepare
en terminale	in year 13, in upper sixth		

le professeur	*teacher*	réussir	*to succeed*
le progrès	*progress*	réussir un examen	*to pass an exam*
rechercher	*to research*	réviser	*to revise*
redoubler	*to resit a year, to stay down a year*	savoir	*to know (a fact)*
		scolaire	*school (adjective)*
le remplaçant	*supply teacher*	le semestre	*semester*
la rentrée	*return (to school)*	le succès Also la réussite	*success*
répéter	*to repeat*		
répondre	*to answer, to reply*	travailler	*to work*
		travailleur	*hardworking*
la réponse	*answer, reply*	le trimestre	*term*
le résultat	*result*		

Higher only:

annulé	*cancelled*	passer en classe supérieure	*to move up a year*
l'assistant de langue (m)	*foreign language assistant*	pédagogique	*teaching, learning*
le car de ramassage	*school bus*	perfectionner	*to improve*
la connaissance	*knowledge*	poser une question	*to ask a question*
debout	*standing*	prononcer	*to pronounce*
se débrouiller	*to manage*	la prononciation	*pronunciation*
deviner	*to guess*	le proviseur	*headteacher*
doué	*talented, gifted*	la rédaction	*essay*
l'échec (m)	*failure*	la rencontre parents-professeurs	*parents' evening*
échouer	*to fail*		
enseigner	*to teach*	se servir de	*to use*
épeler	*to spell*	surchargé	*overloaded*
l'examen final (m)	*final exam*	le surveillant	*supervisor*
l'explication (f)	*explanation*	la tâche	*task*
facultatif	*optional*	la traduction	*translation*

School Rules

absent	*absent*	écouter	*to listen*
apprendre	*to learn*	faire attention	*to be careful, to pay attention*
s'asseoir	*to sit*		
assis	*sitting, seated*	permettre	*to allow*
le bulletin scolaire	*school report*	présent	*present*
défense de	*forbidden to*	le règlement	*rule*
devoir	*to have to, must*	travailler dur	*to work hard*
les devoirs *(m)*	*homework*	l'uniforme *(m)*	*uniform*

Higher only:

l'autorisation *(f)*	*permission*	la retenue	*detention*
écrire des lignes	*to write lines*	sécher les cours	*to play truant*
être en retenue *Also* être collé	*to have detention*	se taire	*to be quiet, to stop talking*
l'injure *(f)*	*insult*		

School Subjects

l'art dramatique *(m)*	*drama*	le français	*French*
les arts ménagers *(m)*	*home economics*	la géographie	*geography*
la biologie	*biology*	l'histoire *(f)*	*history*
la chimie	*chemistry*	l'histoire-géo *(f)*	*history and geography*
le dessin	*art*		
l'éducation physique *(f)*	*PE*	l'informatique *(f)*	*IT, ICT*
les études des médias *(f)*	*media studies*	les langues étrangères *(f)*	*foreign languages*
		le latin	*Latin*

les maths *(f)*	*maths*		la physique	*physics*
Also les mathématiques *(f)*			les sciences *(f)*	*science*
la matière	*subject*		la sociologie	*sociology*
Also le sujet				

Higher only:

l'économie *(f)*	*economics*		les sciences naturelles *(f)*	*biology*
l'instruction religieuse *(f)*	*religious education*		les sciences physiques *(f)*	*physics and chemistry*
les langues vivantes *(f)*	*modern languages*		le thème	*theme, topic*
la matière obligatoire	*compulsory subject*			

School Types and Buildings

la cantine	*canteen*		le laboratoire	*lab(oratory)*
le collège	*secondary school*		le laboratoire de langues	*language lab*
Also l'école secondaire *(f)*			le lycée	*sixth form college*
la cour de récréation	*playground*		le lycée professionnel	*technical college*
l'école *(f)*	*school*		le lycée technique	*technical college*
l'école primaire *(f)*	*primary school*		la maternelle	*nursery school*
l'école privée *(f)*	*private school*		la salle de classe	*classroom*
l'école publique *(f)*	*state school*		la salle de sports	*sports hall*
le hall d'école	*school hall*		la salle des professeurs	*staff room*
l'internat *(m)*	*boarding school*		le terrain de sport	*sports field*

Higher only:

le centre de formation	*training centre*		la salle d'informatique	*computer room*
le pensionnat	*boarding school*			

World of Work

l'apprenti *(m)*	apprentice
Also l'apprentie *(f)*	
l'apprentissage *(m)*	apprenticeship
bénévolement	voluntarily
le boulot	work (familiar)
le candidat	candidate,
Also la candidate	applicant
la carrière	career
le chef	head, boss
le chômage	unemployment
classer	to file
le classeur	file
le collègue	colleague
Also la collègue	
le commerce	business, trade
les compétences *(f)*	skills
les conditions de travail *(f)*	terms of employment
la conférence	conference
la demande d'emploi	job application
le dossier	folder
l'employé *(m)*	employee
Also l'employée *(f)*	
l'employeur *(m)*	employer
enrichissant	enriching
l'entreprise *(f)*	business, company
l'enveloppe *(f)*	envelope
la facture	bill, invoice
faire un stage	to do work experience

la fiche	form
Also le formulaire	
la formation	training
le gérant	manager
Also la gérante	
gérer	to manage
l'heure du déjeuner *(f)*	lunch break
la lettre	letter
livrer	to deliver
mal payé	badly paid
le marketing	marketing
le métier	job
s'occuper de	to look after
par heure	per hour
le patron	boss
Also la patronne	
la pause-café	coffee break
la pause-déjeuner	lunch break
la pause-thé	tea break
poser sa candidature	to apply (for a job)
pressé	in a hurry
la pression	pressure
le produit	product
le propriétaire	owner
Also la propriétaire	
remplir un formulaire	to fill in a form
le salaire	salary
la société	society, company
le stage	course
le stage en entreprise	work experience

le timbre	*stamp*		l'usine *(f)*	*factory*
le travail	*work*		varié	*varied*
le travail bénévole	*charity work*			

Higher only:

s'adresser à	*to speak to*		la lettre de candidature	*cover letter*
l'atelier *(m)*	*workshop*		licencier	*to dismiss, to make redundant*
ci-inclus	*enclosed*		l'offre d'emploi *(f)*	*job advert*
le contrat	*contract*		la possibilité d'avancement	*opportunity for promotion*
l'entretien *(m)*	*interview*			
l'épreuve *(f)*	*test*		qualifié	*qualified*
le fichier	*file*		la réunion	*meeting*
l'impression *(f)*	*impression*		la signature	*signature*
s'inscrire	*to enrol*		suite à	*further to, following*
joindre	*to attach*			

😕 ☐   🙂 ☐   😊 ☐

Notes

Notes

Notes